Masters of Music

ILLUSTRATED BY RICHARD SHIRLEY-SMITH

HANDEL

Masters of Music

HANDEL

Percy M. Young

David White · New York

PUBLISHED IN THE UNITED STATES OF AMERICA BY
DAVID WHITE COMPANY
60 EAST 55TH STREET
NEW YORK, N.Y. 10022
© PERCY M. YOUNG 1966
LIBRARY OF CONGRESS CATALOG CARD NUMBER: 67–16967
PRINTED IN GREAT BRITAIN BY
THE BOWERING PRESS PLYMOUTH

Contents

Preface

HANDEL is one of the greatest of composers. His greatness is best measured by the extent to which his music has become a vital part of the experience of life of all kinds of people, young and old, in many countries. Two countries claim him as their own: Germany and England. He was born in the one and he went to the other as a young man on the threshold of his career; he remained there for the rest of his life. His talents were nurtured in his native land and his techniques were refined in Italy. England, unwittingly, gave him opportunity to put his gifts to their fullest use. He became a national composer; in one sense the greatest English composer of all. Across two hundred years certain works by Handel have taken their place in the pattern of national occasions.

A composer who has achieved this standing has achieved a great deal. He has brought people together, united by a sympathy of which the music is a symbol. Great occasions are one thing; little occasions are another, but no less important. The power of the indestructible music of *Messiah* is apparent even when the performance is amateur and more enthusiastic than efficient. The beauty of a song like "Where-'ere you walk" from *Semele* is still to be marvelled at in an average classroom interpretation. The "Hallelujah" chorus, "See the conquering hero", or the March from *Rinaldo* supply brass bands with continual inspiration.

Handel thus means much to many people, and not only those who describe themselves as "musical". This is because people meant a great deal to him. Among the great composers

Handel was, perhaps, the most sociable. He made and retained friendships, and those who were intimate with him represented a cross-section of society. His interests were wide and his generosity was great. He was a master among musicians, but he was more than a musician. He was, as we would now say, a personality.

In this book we see the musician and the man and we see how the man is his music and the music the man. That is to say when you hear music by Handel it gives some idea of what he was like, while knowledge of the man helps towards an appreciation of the music. There is, I think, one striking feature of Handel's music. It is fresh, direct, approachable, and full of vitality: it has in fact an abiding quality of youth.

P. M. Y.

1. *The Composer of "Messiah"*

IT IS SURPRISING, but it is true, that some musical works make their way to the top of the list of best-sellers without anybody making any particular effort to achieve this ranking. It was the misfortune as well as the fortune of George Frideric Handel to compose a number of works, great and small, which have not only reached the top flight in popular esteem but have stayed there for more than two hundred years. Handel had no objection to being appreciated (no composer has), but he would have preferred a wider range of his music to have won the regard in which a familiar, but limited, selection is held.

The short list well known even to the unmusical contains one complete oratorio, *Messiah*, one "funeral march" from another oratorio (*Saul*), a chorus—"See the conquering hero comes" from a third (*Judas Maccabaeus*), an air, usually known as "Handel's Largo", which comes from the opera *Serse* but is normally performed as though it were "sacred music", and the *Water Music*. There are also a number of songs—sometimes with words that Handel did not know and would not have approved if he had—which are handed out to pupils in secondary schools.

Handel's music has been absorbed into the musical tradition of the English-speaking world, and thousands of people accept it as once upon a time folk-music was accepted. That is, they think very little about the composer who made music which seems so much a part of the way of life. On the other

hand many who do think about Handel find themselves looking at an image that bears little resemblance to the man
himself.

Handel appears to the English as an Englishman who
although born in Germany is among their national heroes; as
a musician who was mainly busy in inventing music suitable
for improving solemn occasions, and the morals and even
the morale of the nation; as one who could quarrel with a
king (or with whom a king could quarrel) and then placate
him by writing engaging pieces to be played by a barge-
borne orchestra on the River Thames.

The personal image is dignified, always dignified. It is of
an elderly bewigged figure, corpulent, and rather remote. It
is sometimes acknowledged that Handel was once a boy. He
was the son of a cross old man—a surgeon—who, it is often
suggested, didn't like music. The unfortunate George
Frideric is pictured as having had to sit in a cold attic practis-
ing a clavichord, or harpsichord, or spinet (according to the
taste of the story-teller) in fear and trembling lest his stern
father should hear a noise that he detested. A most unlikely
tale—as we shall see.

Myths accumulate round great men, for this is one of the
consequences of greatness. But they serve no purpose and
are best removed.

However, from what we do know we can assemble some
facts which will put us on the right road, and show us in
which directions to look in order to establish a more truthful
likeness of one of the most interesting and attractive of men.

Handel composed *Messiah*. This is an oratorio based on
words, from the English Bible, which tell us of the coming of
Christ and His life on earth. The oratorio contains instrumental movements, recitatives, arias and duets for solo
singers, and, above all, choruses. Of the choruses the most

famous is the "Hallelujah" chorus. This oratorio, written by a German who made his home in England, was first performed in Ireland. Some of the music is based on German, some on French, some on Italian, and some on English models. Much of it is strongly Italian and operatic, both in its brilliance and the sometimes florid character of its vocal melody. We know—however dimly—that Handel wrote operas and we see at the top of the printed copies of isolated songs that come our way that their titles are in Italian—*Serse*, *Rinaldo*, *Ariodante*, and so on.

When we listen to the music of Handel we are struck by one thing: it sounds "right". When Handel writes for the voice the music is singable; when he writes for instruments it is playable. At the very least we give him high marks for efficiency. But he is also one of the composers whom we feel able to understand. The musical language is direct and we do not have to clear away a lot of difficulties before we can get at close quarters with the music itself.

All of this is clear in *Messiah*. This is why this work is so widely loved. And not only in English-speaking countries; for I have heard performances in different languages in a number of countries. The result is the same: wherever the audience may be, even if not brought up to the Bible, it is deeply impressed. Handel's greatest musical gift was his ability to make the best use of the most obvious musical terms—in melody, rhythm, and harmony. Yet the general simplicity of his style did not prevent him from describing wide areas of thought and feeling. He knew a lot about the world, and he knew a lot about people. What he had discovered he put into music. But there is more to it than that; for his music, we feel, is intimately connected with affection and concern for humanity. This is what has maintained him in his high place in the common appreciation of music.

2. *Boyhood in Saxony*

THE ANCIENT CITY OF HALLE lies in Saxony, a little way to the west of Leipzig, in the eastern part of Germany. In the seventeenth century, having recovered from the damage caused by the Thirty Years War (1618–48), it was a busy place and prosperous on account of its importance as an industrial and trading centre. The principal manufacture was salt, in later times the foundation of the chemical industry. A little way outside the city, at Weissenfels, the Duke of Saxony had his court. There were other, smaller courts in the neighbourhood too. These added to the prosperity of the city since, needing services of one sort or another, they gave employment. Among those who benefited especially were surgeons, who could adjust their charges to their clients' purses.

The principal surgeon in Halle after the end of the Thirty Years War was Georg Händel (this is the usual German form of the name, which was pronounced Hendel), a tough gentleman noted for his technical skill, his outspokenness, and love of independence.

Georg Händel's first wife died in 1683. Soon afterwards he married again, his second wife, Dorothea Taust, being the daughter of a Lutheran pastor in the nearby village of Giebichenstein. Like many other people in Saxony the Tausts had immigrated from Bohemia during a period of religious persecution. A son was born to Dorothea Händel in 1684, but he died. On February 23, 1685, a second son was born: he was christened Georg Friedrich, according to the Lutheran rites, in the great church in the Market Place in which Martin Luther had once preached.

4

As a boy Händel had his opportunities. He could meet
the most interesting people in a lively city because of his
father's many contacts. He could sometimes enjoy journeys
into the countryside in his father's coach when the old man
(he was 63 when Georg Friedrich was born) was making a
professional visit. Or he could walk along the river Saale to
Giebichenstein where, under the shadow of the ancient
castle, his grand-parents lived. There was a good grammar
school in Halle, and the University had famous teachers. It
was a musical town, in which one of the greatest of seventeenth-century composers had lived and worked. This was
Samuel Scheidt (1587–1654). In half a dozen of the medieval
churches, now Lutheran, there were good organists who
regularly gave performances of church cantatas—with solo
singers and an orchestra got together from among the muni-
cipal musicians. And in the medieval cathedral, once monas-
tic but since the Reformation a Calvinist church, there was
an excellent organ. From time to time the civic musicians

5

gave performances of their own. Best of all, perhaps, from a boy's point of view, were those given by the brass players from the bridge joining the two spires of Our Lady's Church that rode high over the Market Place. It might seem that Händel's later skill in the most effective use of brass instruments stemmed from this early experience.

It was not out of the ordinary for a boy in seventeenth-century Germany to like music, for it provided an important and exciting part of the pattern of life. George Händel was the surgeon to the Court at Weissenfels where there was a good deal of music. On one occasion when Georg Friedrich went with his father the Duke heard him playing the organ and observed that he semed to have some talent that would appear to him to deserve the attention of a good teacher. The organist of the Market Church in Halle, Friedrich Wilhelm Zachau (1663–1712), was a very good teacher. He was also a very good composer, especially of church cantatas. It was very convenient to send Georg Friedrich to Zachau, for he worked only five minutes' walk away from the Händels' comfortable house in St Nicholas's Street.

In learning the craft of composition the young musician listens to as many works as he can. The influence of the earliest music that he hears remains with him always and from time to time is liable to show as the mature composer unconsciously remembers and reproduces what had long been tucked away in his memory. There is a song in the opera *Rinaldo* which is well-known in various versions with English words:

1a.

Behind this there was, however, the shape of a German folk-song:

In a cantata of Zachau this passage appears:

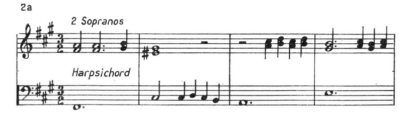

In a Sarabande from a Suite in D minor for harpsichord we find Handel writing:

So the music that he heard when he was a boy carried through into Handel's later years.

Georg Friedrich learned to play the harpsichord, the organ, the violin, and the oboe. In later life he said that the oboe was then his favourite instrument and at the age of ten he had already composed a set of oboe sonatas (subsequently lost). His chief exercise was to write a church cantata once a week. Since at this time there was no knowing what his ultimate career would be he had other homework as well. His studies in the main were classical, but he learned to write German poetry and to understand much in the field of theology. Music, however, gradually assumed the greatest importance. On a visit to Berlin (the principal city of the state of Prussia to which Halle now belonged) Georg Friedrich made a good impression on the Elector, who told his father that he might well follow a musical career.

Georg Händel died in 1697 and his son wrote and published an ode in his memory. Five years went by and Georg Friedrich matriculated as a student of the University. It was intended that he should study law, a convenient foundation for most professions in those days. In his first year at the University, however, the post of organist at the cathedral fell vacant and Händel was successful in his application to fill the vacancy. He gave up his other studies and became a full-time musician. He was encouraged to do so by Georg Philipp Telemann (1681–1767), a brilliant young man from Magdeburg, who, although nominally a student of law in Leipzig, was intending to follow a career in music. Telemann, who was to become one of the greater German musicians, had a persuasive tongue and an attractive personality. Händel enjoyed his company and their friendship was life-long.

Händel and Telemann talked much about music—about the church cantatas that were a German speciality; about the keyboard sonatas and fugues of Johann Kuhnau (1660–1722) —Bach's predecessor as Cantor of St Thomas's Church in Leipzig; about the instrumental and vocal music—some specially composed for student societies—of Johann Rosenmüller (1620–84), of the ducal town of Wolfenbüttel; about

the *concerti grossi* of the Italian master Arcangelo Corelli (1653–1713); about the French overtures of Jean-Baptiste Lully (1632–87) and André Campra (1660–1744) that could be found at many German Courts at which French culture had been implanted by Dukes who imitated the practices made fashionable by Louis XIV. In one way or another the works of all these (as well as other) composers helped the eager apprentice composers to find out how to develop their own ideas.

Halle and Leipzig were pleasant places in which to live. There was plenty of musical activity and one could certainly do well enough in them. Telemann and Händel, however, were ambitious and, aiming high, saw that if they were to get anywhere near the summit of their ambitions they must travel. The fashionable cult in European music was opera. Anyone who hoped to achieve celebrity as a composer must learn how to write an opera in the Italian style. This meant leaving home and going south to Dresden, or north to Hanover, Brunswick, or Hamburg. Händel chose to go to Hamburg by way of Hanover. Behind this decision lay the advice of Telemann who spoke of the skill, influence, and importance of Agostino Steffani (1654–1728), priest, diplomat, and composer. Steffani was a high official at the Court of the Elector of Hanover. He knew everybody, and the sooner a young man made his acquaintance the better.

3. *Travels*

IN THE SUMMER of 1703 Händel, having called at Hanover, arrived in Hamburg, where the opera was directed by Reinhard Keiser (1674–1739). Keiser, composer of more than a hundred operas, was renowned throughout Germany, not least of all because it seemed that he might develop a genuinely German style of opera. Händel found a post as a second violinist in Keiser's orchestra and from this modest vantage-point took a look round. He played all the organs he could find, went to as many concerts as he could engineer invitations to, and enjoyed the choral performances in the City's churches. He made friends with Johann Mattheson (1681–1764), already an opera composer and destined to be famous both as musician and writer on music. The general spread of interest in music and the lives of musicians in those days is shown by a new departure in the production of books and articles of a more popular nature. Mattheson was a pioneer in this field.

Händel and Mattheson worked together and played together. They once fought a duel after a sudden, heated quarrel. They went north to Lübeck to see if either of them stood a chance of succeeding the great Dietrich Buxtehude (1637–1707). If either had been willing to marry Buxtehude's daughter Anna he would have been given the organistship in Lübeck; but neither was willing. Back in Hamburg Händel gave music lessons to the family of the English representative in the city, John Wich. He composed works which included a setting of the Passion story and two operas. Neither *Almira* nor *Nero* was successful, but the fact that

11

they had been produced at all was an incentive to further enterprise, and Händel decided that now was the time to go to Italy.

His social instincts were strong and he made friends easily; thus it was that at the crucial moment Händel was able to persuade Prince Giovanni Gastone de' Medici to help him towards an excursion to Italy. This Prince, whose wife was German, was the son of the Grand Duke of Tuscany, and an ardent amateur musician. He was useful in giving advice, and possibly financial assistance, to Händel, who therefore went straight to Florence with an introduction to Giovanni Gastone's brother, Ferdinando. The chief musician at the Florentine Court was Alessandro Scarlatti (*c.* 1659–1725), one of the most important musicians of the day.

Italy was then very cosmopolitan. Visitors came from all parts of Europe to study the arts, to polish their manners, to be able to go home and to say that they had been to Italy. Most of the musicians employed at the courts and in the theatres were naturally Italian, but not all. A good orchestral player could always find a job, or a patron, or both. Händel aimed high. He would try his luck as a composer. In between completing settings of two Psalms and other church music, to Latin words, for the Carmelites in Rome and—so it was said—falling in and out of love, Händel completed his opera *Rodrigo*. After a satisfactory reception of this work in Florence Händel travelled to Venice, where he met Domenico Scarlatti (1685–1757), son of Alessandro. The younger Scarlatti was a virtuoso harpsichordist and composer of sonatas for that instrument; the elder was one of the great opera and cantata composers of the period, and the perfecter of the form of the *aria*.

Händel was a quick learner and ready to acclimatise his style to the company he was keeping. In Italy he wrote with great fluency in the current Italian manner. But it was not only music that compelled his attention. He collected acquaintances who were drawn to him by his vivid interest in whatever went on in the world, by his ready Saxon humour—for the Saxons like the Anglo-Saxons have a marked sense of humour, by his evident friendliness, and by his enthusiasms. Händel made friends among the Italians but also among those of other nations who were to be found in Italy. There were numerous Englishmen about. Händel met the Earl of Manchester in Venice. He also met Ernest of Hanover, brother of the future George I of England.

From Venice Händel went again to Rome and was lionised by those among the Cardinals who were the principal protectors of culture in the City. In Rome he composed two oratorios, to fit into the programmes of his host, the Prince Francesco Ruspoli. These oratorios, to Italian texts, were *La resurrezione* (*The Resurrection*) and *Il trionfo del tempo e del disinganno* (*The Triumph of Time and Truth*). At this time he was also much in the company of Arcangelo Corelli, whose *concerti grossi* were the most celebrated and advanced orchestral works of the period. Composers from all over Europe studied Corelli's method of handling the concerto form and also the string ensemble (with a group of solo instruments called *concertino* and a main body of players which was the *concerto grosso*) for which he wrote so brilliantly and went home to write in a similar vein. The influence of Corelli is strong in Handel's *Concerti grossi*, most of all in the great set of twelve (Op. 6) composed in 1739.

After visiting Naples, where he wrote a pastoral piece on the classical story of Acis and Galatea, Händel returned to an opera project for which the libretto had been prepared by Cardinal Grimani. This opera was *Agrippina*. He had a fine cast of singers, which included the fourteen-year-old Margherita Durastanti and Giuseppe Boschi, the celebrated bass who had already sung for Händel in Naples. *Agrippina* brought the house down. It ran for a month, and at the end of the performances the excited and generous Italians called out *"Viva il caro Sassone"* ("Long live the dear Saxon"). Händel had triumphed where it was most difficult to succeed, in Italy—the home of opera and of opera composers. And all this before his twenty-fifth birthday.

4. *Arrival in England*

HÄNDEL LEFT ITALY on a triumphant note and went back to
Hanover, where he was appointed to succeed Steffani as
Kapellmeister (Director of Music). Since his predecessor had
not been content to remain in one place Händel saw no
reason why he should not have freedom of movement. In the
summer of 1710 he went home to see his mother and his
sisters. Then he went across Germany to Düsseldorf and
paid his respects to the sister-in-law of Gastone and Ferdinando de' Medici, who, as Electress, had her court there.

From Düsseldorf he travelled to London—for many
foreign musicians a veritable Mecca. London had many
attractions. It was a rich city, in which many of the well-to-do
—many knowledgeable and genuinely interested, some
anxious to keep up with the Joneses—were ready to subsi-
dise the arts. It was a beautiful city since its rebuilding by
Sir Christopher Wren—St Paul's Cathedral was ready for
dedication in 1710 and, standing white and vast at the top
of Ludgate Hill, it seemed to typify the confidence and
stability of the city and country. London attracted those, like
Händel, who valued their personal independence. Johann
Christoph Pepusch (1667–1752), for instance, had left
Prussia because he had been horrified by the arbitrary act of
the Elector in having an army officer executed without trial,
and had made his home in England. Composers and performers had long been in the habit of regarding England as
a country in which foreigners were welcomed and, if they
were lucky, amply rewarded. From the time of the Restora-
tion they had come in large numbers, and well-known Ger-

man composers, Gottfried Finger, Gerhard Diesineer, and August Kühnel among them, had furnished material for the concert clubs which were a feature of London life. Finger had so well established himself that he not only composed for the London theatres but also for the traditional annual St Cecilia's Day celebrations. Händel in visiting London was doing no more than many other of his countrymen who practised the same profession.

Yet maybe there was more to it. English music was not

quite unknown in distant Halle in the seventeenth century. Pieces by Jacobean composers were in instrumental part-books and there Samuel Scheidt, the "father" of Halle music, had once written a set of variations on a melody by John Dowland. William Brade, a fine instrumental composer, had indeed lived and worked for a time in Halle, and his daughter had married a local surgeon: one of the surgeons to whom Georg Händel was once an apprentice. And in the course of his travels Georg Friedrich had met a number of Englishmen.

Arrived in London Händel, as usual, made social contacts. He was introduced to Sir John Stanley, a court official, and to Stanley's ten-year-old niece, Mary Granville. Mary fell in love with her uncle's young and attractive German guest, and, she said, then determined to play the harpsichord as well as he did. In fact she never achieved this ambition; but she, and her brother Bernard, became life-long friends of the composer. Händel also met Aaron Hill, poet and manager of the Haymarket Theatre, and was commissioned by him to provide an opera for his company. This was *Rinaldo*, the most splendid opera a London public had ever seen. Full of life, colour, brilliance, and with a tremendous feeling for characterisation *Rinaldo* was an enormous success.

After *Rinaldo* Händel lingered on in London, meeting all the amateur musicians—some aristocrats, some civil servants, some tradesmen—who were in the habit of meeting weekly in Clerkenwell on the premises of Thomas Britton. He was a coal-merchant, who organised the meetings and possessed the finest private collection of music in London. Britton, rough-mannered and eccentric, was greatly loved and he did a great deal to make music a recreation for the many rather than the few. But Händel eventually remembered that he was Director of Music at Hanover and re-crossed the Channel—with a set of duets composed for the Princess Caroline.

To salve his conscience he also composed some oboe concertos and cantatas.

In 1712 Händel was once again in London, with two operas, *Il pastor fido* (The faithful shepherd) and *Teseo* (Theseus). The libretto of the second was written by Nicola Haym who was musical director to the Duke of Bedford, and acquainted with the art-loving Earl of Burlington to whom the libretto of *Teseo* was inscribed. Burlington held concerts at his town house; so did others of the nobility. Händel was invited to take part in these concerts and thus secured his base in England.

One of the occupations of an English composer was writing music to celebrate national occasions. Purcell had done this brilliantly. But alas! Purcell had died in 1695. There was now no native composer of that calibre. William Croft (1678–1727), organist of Westminster Abbey, was a good but conservative composer who would do a solid but not inspiring job. When he knew that there were to be celebrations at St Paul's in 1713 in honour of the Peace of Utrecht (which marked the end of the War of Spanish Succession) Händel looked at the *Te Deum* and *Jubilate* which Purcell had written twenty years earlier, to make sure that he knew the kind of music expected, and composed his *Utrecht Te Deum*. But before this was performed he had written a *Birthday Ode* (a kind of cantata) for Queen Anne's birthday. The Queen was delighted, and settled on the grateful composer a pension of £200 a year.

On August 14, 1714, Queen Anne died, to be succeeded by George Lewis, Elector of Hanover, and great-grandson of James I of England, as George I. The new King brought so many of his Hanoverian subjects to his new realm that the London Society became thoroughly Anglo-German. In comparison with the newcomers Händel, who had an ear for

languages and had studied English, and had made friends
with poets and writers, might almost pass as an Englishman!
He was, of course, still a servant of the Court of Hanover.
But nobody seems to have been particularly bothered about
that. *The Water Music* was not written to put things right;
indeed it was not to be written for another three years and
then simply as suitable entertainment for a royal excursion
on the Thames. Many other composers had written such sets
of suites for other similar occasions.

When the Hanoverian invasion took place Händel was
planning another opera, from which he turned aside to
arrange another production of *Rinaldo* in honour of the
Coronation.

5. *The Opera House*

OPERA, which in the modern sense may be said to have begun its career a little less than a century before Händel was born, was, as has been shown already, an Italian invention. The Italian manner spread across Europe but its progress was halted by the English Channel. During the seventeenth century English composers were much more inclined to add music to plays than they were to unite a specially written libretto with music into a "drama through music" as the Italians called it. Purcell wrote magnificent dramatic music, but—with the exception of *Dido and Aeneas* and, to a point, *King Arthur*, his works which are called operas are not. Now the English people (or those who counted in these matters) had no desire to be thought backward in matters of culture. The Earl of Burlington, to take one of Händel's acquaintances, was a student of art, architecture, literature, and music, and he was in the habit of inviting artists and interested amateurs to his house to discuss problems in all the arts, and he set up as a patron in quite a big way. Opera, however, depended on opera houses, and opera houses could only in those days be built and staffed by a court. England only had one court, and, being answerable to Parliament, a fairly parsimonious one at that. Thus whatever opera there was in the early years of the eighteenth century was imported, and the really expert singers—the stars, who could command enormous fees—were also imported.

Opera was art; it was also entertainment. It was without any kind of official support and wholly dependent on the box-office. The problems facing an opera composer wishing to

make a career in England were formidable. Händel thought the risk worth taking (since he could also earn money in other ways and in any case had his steady pension), and for more than twenty years was first and foremost a composer of operas to be sung in Italian by mixed teams of Italian, German, French, and British singers, to English audiences who mostly did not understand a word of what was going on. But ignorance is frequently happily carried by those who wish to give the impression of being cultured.

Anyone who wishes to be a composer must be tough; an opera composer (who has to deal with many often "temperamental" people) must be tougher. Händel, a born optimist, was very tough. He was also very good at getting his own way.

Altogether Händel composed some forty operas, the great majority of them for London. From this number one might notice *Rinaldo, Amadigi* (1715), *Radamisto* (1720), *Ottone* (1722), *Giulio Cesare* (1724), *Rodelinda* (1725), *Admeto* (1727), *Tolomeo* (1728), *Poro* and *Alessandro* (1731), *Orlando* (1733), and *Ariodante* (1735) as being the best. A large number of songs from the operas are fortunately available in English versions (N.B. *Arias from the operas of G. F. Handel*; O.U.P.). The operas are to be found in the repertoires of some German opera-houses today and there they may be appreciated in their proper setting. The stories are complicated and often fantastic and absurd (but not more so than those of many films), and are best read up in advance. But the power of the music is such that it can overcome improbabilities of plot.

Händel impresses the listener by his perception of the qualities of different kinds of voices, by the way in which he can range from the simple *siciliano* or minuet type of aria to one of extreme but always manageable brilliance; by his talent for marrying a vocal line to a frequently varied instrumental accompaniment; by the evocative quality of his incidental orchestral music; and by his quick recognition of the essential points in a landscape, in a personality, or in a dramatic situation. The subjects of the operas are, according to precedent, "heroic", and the scenes are usually set in distant and unfamiliar countries. Yet out of his historic figures Händel makes living persons, and his scenic music might well refer to familiar landscapes. This was because he had the gift of clear statement.

But simplicity of statement did not mean that he did not see and expound the shape of great human problems. Jealousy, as between the principal women characters in *Rinaldo* and *Teseo*; distress, as shown by the unhappy Polissena of *Radamisto* when she discovers the unfaithfulness of her husband; madness as in the famous 5/8 movement in *Orlando*; the thought of death enshrined in Tolomeo's aria "Stille amare": all these ideas, with their attendant sadnesses, are put before the listener. This is how "Stille amare" is introduced by the orchestra; the feeling of sadness is shown in the semitone shifts in the bass:

3.
Larghetto

But they are shown against the more cheerful and tender sides of life. For lightness of mood it is difficult to find a better example than the Minuet from *Alcina*, with its athletic leaps in the melody: one may almost see the ballet dancers Händel had in mind when he wrote this opera:

4.

Minuet

Thus we may begin to see how Händel gives us human personality in the round. The operas may only rarely be seen outside of Germany. Fortunately, however, Händel transferred his techniques, impressions, and intentions into a new medium: that of oratorio. He did not want to do this. He was compelled to by force of circumstances, and, it may be said, by the opinions and counsel of friendly advisers.

Händel was mightily industrious. He would scour Europe looking for singers for the opera. In 1716, for instance, he went to Dresden, taking advantage of the journey to visit his mother and family in Halle, and other friends in Hamburg and Anspach. Having maintained his connection with Hamburg through Mattheson he was able to deliver a setting of the *Passion* which he had composed for performance there. At Anspach he met an old friend, Johann Christoph Schmidt. Händel was sorry to find Schmidt in poor circumstances and took him and his family to London, where Schmidt became Händel's secretary and copyist. Later on Schmidt's son succeeded him in these useful offices. It was an onerous undertaking, for Händel always wrote at enormous speed and his manuscripts are anything but legible.

In 1719 Händel was again in Germany looking for singers. This was a sad visit, for in the previous year his sister Dorothea, married to a Prussian government official, had died. In 1729 he was in Italy and then again in Germany, where he found his mother blind and infirm. In none of these Germany visits did Händel meet Bach. This looks odder now than it would have seemed then. Händel was busy and when in Germany had little time for anything but his business commitments and his family. And Bach, after all, was not then regarded with the veneration which attached to him after his death. He was well-known as a fine organist, but his compositions were familiar only to a few.

In respect of opera Händel was single-minded. This was the kind of music he wanted to write, and it was this he could compose best. But despite many moments of triumph he was following a lost cause. Opera in England depended on its private subscribers. From time to time the nobility put money into it and in 1720 formed a "Royal Academy of Music" for its organisation. But they quarrelled among themselves, and in one year, 1721, an opposition group put up a rival composer to Händel. This was an Italian, Giovanni Battista Buononcini (1670–1755). After eight years of rather chequered activity the Royal Academy packed up.

If an unsatisfactory financial background was one hazard another was the behaviour of star singers. The Italian singers were often extremely tiresome. Vain, arrogant, greedy, they aroused the distaste of the English and the frequent anger of Händel. Least of all could the English tolerate the male sopranos and altos whose particular quality of voice resulted from an outrageous surgical operation. In 1727 two famous female singers Faustina Bordoni (who later married the German composer Hasse) and Francesca Cuzzoni let their jealousy of each other grow to such a pitch that they ended a performance of an opera by Buononcini by fighting on the stage.

C

Then there was the matter of language. During the early years of the reign of George I the English, put off perhaps by a German-speaking court, developed a fit of patriotism and began to chafe at having to try to understand languages to which they were not brought up. What, they said, was the use of paying good money to go to the theatre to hear an opera with words that were unintelligible. What was wrong with English? Italian opera was clearly an uncertain prospect. In 1728 it became even more uncertain, for in that year the satirical *Beggar's Opera* of John Gay (with music taken from familiar folk-tunes and popular pieces by Purcell and Händel) was produced by John Rich at Lincoln's Inn Fields theatre. The *Beggar's Opera* suited public taste, and it has done so ever since. Händel, who was a friend of Gay, enjoyed it, even though the prison scene in the *Beggar's Opera* was intended to parody the prison scenes that were such a familiar part of Händel's own operas, and even though his March from *Rinaldo* was one of the hits.

Händel lost a good deal of money which he had invested in operatic undertakings. But he was never bankrupt. This was a legend maintained for many years by people who thought that musicians produced better music when they were kept in a state of poverty. We know that Händel was not bankrupt because his account in the Bank of England, which may still be seen, disproves the legend.

6. *Friends*

OPERA WAS A VERY IMPORTANT PART of Händel's musical life, but it was not the whole of it. He had the ability to do a number of things at the same time. Thus during the first years of his residence in England the list of his works grew in many directions.

In the eighteenth century a composer produced music as it was wanted. On the whole he did not sit down and write a piece hoping that some day it would be hailed as a masterpiece. He lived in the present and was content to let the future take care of itself. At the same time a composer depended very much on his friends, who would encourage, advise, and criticise. Influential friends could also arrange for performances of works to take place. One of the striking things about Händel is the number of friends he had. Some were persons of rank; others were of more modest station. Händel treated them all as equals.

When he had been in England for some years Händel became Director of Music (part-time) to the Duke of Chandos, who had made a fortune out of the War of Spanish Succession, built a palace at Canons north of London, and lived on the grand scale. Händel wrote for Canons a set of anthems —which were on a larger scale than most English anthems and in form rather nearer to church cantatas. These were called the *Chandos Anthems* and showed how well Händel understood not only solo voices but also the choral ensemble. Encouraged by the opportunities at Canons Händel wrote two other important works. One was *Acis and Galatea*, a "pastoral cantata"; the kind of work that went down well on festive occasions at Italian courts. But this was to an English text, and a beautiful one at that. The author was John Gay, who had borrowed passages from another of Händel's acquaintances, Alexander Pope, whom the composer had got to know through Lord Burlington. In preparing this work Händel listened to the literary arguments not only of Gay and Pope but also another poet, John Hughes.

Introducing the chorus "Happy we" in *Acis and Galatea* we find an orchestral passage, or *ritornello*, which closely resembles a Welsh folk-melody. As it happens when Händel was busy on this work he numbered among his acquaintances the court harpist, named Powel, who was given a part to play in *Haman and Mordecai*. Powel, who inspired later works by Händel, was a Welshman, and it is likely that he played to the composer some of his country's music. Händel liked the harp and he wrote a concerto in which it was the solo instrument. This was published together with the organ concertos (Opus 4) of 1738. This passage work from the first movement shows how well the arrangement of notes suited the instrument, and insofar as the bass is concerned how economical Händel was with his musical material.

5.

In 1720, soon after *Acis and Galatea* was written, Händel brought out another work with English words. This was a so-called masque, based on a Bible story, and entitled *Haman and Mordecai* (later the title was changed to Esther).

This work owed something to the French dramatist Racine who had written a play on the same subject, something again to Pope, and something to another industrious, if minor poet, Samuel Humphreys. Another literary friend of this period was the Scottish doctor John Arbuthnot, a versatile man, physician to Queen Anne, and one of Händel's most loyal supporters. It was said that Arbuthnot too had a hand in the preparation of the text for *Haman and Mordecai*.

For the performance of the work Händel hired the singers of the Chapel Royal. Among them was one who remembered taking part in this performance and whose pride and pleasure was, as we shall see, later turned to good account. This was Bernard Gates, whose name may be seen in Händel's own note of the soloists on the manuscript of the eighth Chandos Anthem in the British Museum. As for the Duke of Chandos he so far forgot himself as to present Händel with £1,000 for his work on this piece: considering the value of money in those days this was a most generous gift.

At this point Händel bought a handsome house in Lower Brook Street, near St George's Church, Hanover Square (at which he worshipped for the rest of his life). This was a fashionable and convenient part of London and Händel was able to entertain his friends and to rehearse his artists in comfort. Among his intimate friends were Aaron Hill, the theatrical manager, who was also an experienced dramatist; James Quin, an Irish actor who excelled in the Shakespearean roles of Othello, Falstaff, and Lear; and Mrs Pendarves— Mary Granville whom Händel had first met as a little girl— and her brother Bernard. Händel used to take round sketches of his music and play them to Mrs Pendarves. Sometimes she would persuade him to give an informal concert in her drawing-room, when he would play the harpsichord suites which showed his great skill as a performer so effectively.

In the eighteenth century those who could afford to do
so ate well. Händel could and did. His appetite, though not
exceptional by the standards of those days, was the subject of
censure by those who could not fault Händel otherwise.
Among those who did not like Händel was the artist Joseph
Goupy, who had once painted scenes for the Royal Academy
operas. Goupy paid off some old score when in 1730 he
drew a notorious and unkind cartoon, showing a pig-like
Händel eating vast quantities of food. This cartoon passed
into the Händel mythology, so that some people remembered
his alleged gluttony when they had forgotten both his music
and his great human qualities.

7. *A British Subject*

A MAN'S NATIONALITY BY BIRTH is one matter over which he has no control. Händel was born a German and in that sense he died a German. He maintained his connections with his native land throughout his life and was ever concerned about the welfare of his friends and relations, a number of whom were generously remembered in his Will. But he had that rare and valuable capacity of being able to live with people, as one of them and not as a stranger, wherever he happened to be. We have seen how in Italy he enjoyed being welcomed into Italian society and the quality of his sympathy for the cultural way of living he found there is reflected in his Italian music. It was, however, in England that he discovered how best he could make use of his talents. It was here too that he found the greatest appreciation of his versatility, and at the same time most positive form of those ideals by which he was inspired as a citizen.

Händel believed in the principle of a monarchy (in the eighteenth century he really had no alternative), but preferred monarchy when its powers were, as in England but not in Hanover, held in check by parliament. As music master to the royal family and as an official composer he was frequently in close contact with exalted persons. But he addressed them, as he also addressed the nobility, without reserve. If the Prince of Wales arrived late at a rehearsal Händel showed his irritation, so that the poor Princess of Wales had to say to the entourage, "Hush! Hush! Händel's in a passion." To behave like that was possible in England without any suggestion of disrespect: it was not possible in

Europe in general. Händel found at an early stage of his life in England that liberty and independence could be preserved better there than in many countries. The case should not be overstated. It always requires courage to retain genuine independence in any society, but in some more than in others the climate is helpful. Händel was ready to fight for his own independence at all times; but he was also prepared to accept the fact that others were entitled to their independence.

Unlike some composers Händel had a keen business sense. This he needed to have insofar as his activities in the fields of opera and, later, oratorio depended on his own initiative and his own capital. Sometimes he made money. Sometimes he lost money. On balance he came out very well and he shrewdly invested his profits in South Sea Annuities. His faith in the integrity of the English financial and mercantile world was one reason for his willing acceptance of English conditions. There were others. Under the government of Sir Robert Walpole the country was kept out of wars so that its prosperity increased considerably. The stability of society was further supported by the absence of religious disorder. The Church of England did not differ very greatly from the Lutheran Church into which Händel had been baptized, and he felt at ease with its liturgy and customs. English cultural life, though heavily weighted on the side of literature, was stimulating and, such as it was, was woven into the social fabric.

All in all Händel found himself at ease in England and, even though he spoke English with a Saxon accent, he felt like an Englishman. More and more the English felt that he was an Englishman. Apart from the fact that those who knew him well liked him and felt no barrier to exist his name became increasingly known throughout the country. The newspapers noted performances of his works and John Walsh, the most enterprising publisher of the day, issued them as soon as he could get hold of fair copies from which his editions could be engraved. When Händel learned how Walsh had made a fortune out of *Rinaldo* he said that next time Walsh should compose the opera and he would publish it.

In the course of fifteen years Händel's music became indispensable. Tunes from his operas and concertos and his chamber music works were familiar at private music gatherings all over the country. Public occasions required his anthems and other church music and the movements of his *Water Music*—that set of pieces he had written in 1717—and his marches. In London Händel visited St Paul's Cathedral to play the organ, and to go to the nearest taverns with the organist, Dr Maurice Greene, and the singing-men for more informal music-making. Near the Haymarket Theatre there were Hickford's Rooms at which fashionable concerts were given. Händel was often to be seen there.

In 1726 he felt that he should show his respect for the English people by petitioning to become a naturalised citizen. At the end of his petition to the House of Lords Händel wrote his name as George Frideric Handel, which is the style now used in England. On February 20, 1726, King George I approved the Bill which made Handel's request effective.

8. *Oratorio*

A FEW OF THE GREAT COMPOSERS showed exceptional talents when very young. Although some, such as Mozart, were "infant prodigies" it is not to be taken for granted (although it sometimes is) that all composers of genius belonged to this class. Handel's development was steady rather than spectacular and while his achievement was considerable by the time he took English nationality at the age of forty-one his best known works—in almost every field—were yet to come.

A year after George I had confirmed Handel's British citizenship and appointed him to the post of Court composer, for which he was now eligible, he died and was succeeded by George II. In October, 1727, the Coronation took place and Handel composed four anthems to celebrate the occasion. In these pieces for voices and orchestra which are familiar to present-day choirs Handel again shows how brilliantly he could translate a national mood into terms of music. The autumn festivities of that year kept him busy. He had to compose pieces for the court balls and also to stage an opera. This was *Riccardo primo, re d'Inghilterra* (*Richard I, King of England*). It was, in a general way, obviously a suitable subject, for—even with Italian words—it aroused deep-seated patriotic feelings. At the same time the supremacy of Italian opera was nearing its end.

In 1732 Bernard Gates, now Master of the Chapel Royal Choristers, brought the largest of Handel's works of the Canons period out of storage and gave a performance of *Esther* (formerly *Haman and Mordecai*) at his house in honour of Handel's birthday. This performance being welcomed by those who attended Gates arranged another, for a meeting of the Academy of Ancient Music of which he was a leading member, in the Crown and Anchor Tavern. Two more performances followed in the next few weeks, the second taking place in the King's Theatre, Haymarket, on May 2.

The advertisement for this performance ended with this note: "There will be no acting on the stage, but the house will be fitted up in a decent manner, for the audience. The Musick to be disposed after the manner of the Coronation service." By the "Musick" was meant the solo singers (who were borrowed from the opera-house), the choir—of the Chapel Royal, and the orchestra. As in the opera-house the orchestra consisted basically of the string group—of first and second violins, violas, 'cellos, and double-basses—with harpsichord, oboes and bassoons. Sometimes the oboe-players changed to the flute when the composer required that tone-colour; trumpets and drums were available for ceremonial or noisy effects, such as were associated with soldiers and war-like scenes; the organ, a small chamber-instrument, was useful from time to time; and Handel added harp and lute when he felt so inclined. Handel in fact had a keen perception of the evocative quality of orchestral sounds and he made remarkable use of what he had.

That there was "no acting on the stage" when *Esther* was performed at the Haymarket Theatre was due to the refusal of the Dean of the Chapel Royal to allow his choristers to be mixed up with anything that was patently theatrical. Since actors and actresses and opera singers were not notable for respectability it is not surprising that the Dean (who was also Bishop of London) acted as he did. *Esther*, however, was approved—especially by the King and the court. Seeing the way the wind was blowing the father of Thomas Augustine Arne (1710–78) put on a performance of *Acis and Galatea*

without asking Handel's permission, in order to give an opportunity to his eighteen-year-old daughter Susanna who was a promising young soprano. Handel was not pleased and countered it with a performance under his own direction. Towards the end of that year Aaron Hill wrote to Handel asking that the composer should "be resolute enough to deliver us from an Italian bondage, and demonstrate that English is soft enough for opera. . . ."

Handel, however, did not see a future for English opera; but he did for the new type of work—opera without action and based on plots taken from the Old Testament. Because there was no movement on the stage Handel could make much more use of the chorus (opera choruses were generally brief and perfunctory). This suited him. It also suited his public, for choral music was very much part of the Englishman's experience of music. The public was also liable to approve anything connected, however remotely, with the English Bible. Handel made a shrewd judgment. And when it came to selecting plots from the Old Testament he went first to those that were just as exciting as those to be found in opera.

He called in his old collaborator Samuel Humphreys and told him to get on with a libretto for *Deborah*. This story from the *Book of Judges* is dramatic, and Handel set it to dramatic music. Working in a hurry—he always did—he used up some of the Coronation anthem *The King shall rejoice* and some of the *Passion* music he had written for Hamburg. *Deborah*, which was mistakenly described by one newspaper as an opera, was performed in Lent, 1733. In the summer *Athaliah*, also to a text by Humphreys, was performed in Oxford, where Handel had been invited by the university authorities. This was a profitable visit, for he was also able to arrange a whole series of concerts in the city. Meanwhile others were beginning to hope that they might reap where Handel had sown. William Defesch (d. 1758), leader of the band at Marylebone Gardens, composed the oratorio *Judith*, which, however, is not remembered for its music but on account of the caricature of a performance that William Hogarth drew. Hogarth, a keen enough musician to be a member of the Academy of Vocal Music, was a friend of Handel's. Then there was Niccola Porpora (1686–1767), brought to England by the nobility as an operatic rival to Handel: he composed an oratorio, *David*, in 1734. It was, however, said to be "not equal to Mr Handel's oratorio of *Esther* or *Deborah*". So reported Mrs Pendarves.

The right time of the year for oratorio was Lent, for then opera was forbidden on Wednesdays and Fridays. A similar restriction had in France led in 1725 to the institution of the *Concert Spirituel* ("Spiritual Concert"), consisting of vocal and instrumental music of the highest quality. The oratorio as Handel developed it was part opera (and always advertised as in 3 Acts), part anthem—with stress on the chorus, and part concert. Handel was a fine organist. Therefore for the better entertainment of his supporters he wrote organ concertos which he played between the acts of his oratorios. This was a novelty in 1735, but afterwards it became a consistent part of the programme, and other kinds of concertos were also added to the oratorio evenings.

At the end of 1735 Handel, finding that the new form that had evolved was very congenial, departed from a Bible text and made a setting of Dryden's *Alexander's Feast*. At the beginning of the second act of this work he gave a notable and characteristic example of his feeling for orchestral colour by writing a ghostly introduction for violas, three bassoons, 'cellos, basses, and organ, to a passage about "a ghostly band ... [of] Grecian ghosts that in battle were slain".

6.

Alexander's Feast was performed at Covent Garden Theatre (which Handel had hired two years previously when an opposing faction of the nobility had made it impossible for him to renew a lease of the Haymarket) on February 19, 1736. Two months later he had to produce another of his many ceremonial works, an anthem for the wedding of the Prince of Wales to the Princess Augusta of Saxe Gotha. Handel performed this task with somewhat mixed feelings, for the Prince—largely to spite his father—had supported Giovanni Buononcini, when that composer had been brought to London as a rival to Handel.

In 1736 Handel found that in the field of opera there was yet another competitor, in the person of Johann Adolph Hasse (1699–1783), the director of opera at Dresden and the husband of one of Handel's former singers, Faustina Bordoni. But still Handel persevered with his operas. In 1737 *Arminio* and *Giustino* were produced, but during Lent there were performances of *Esther*, *Alexander's Feast*, and a revised version of an Italian work of 1708 now called *The Triumph of Time and Truth*.

Since Handel not only wrote the music of his operas and oratorios but also chose and rehearsed the singers and directed the performances, and since he had a host of other things to attend to, including the composition of instrumental works, and solo performances as harpsichordist or organist, it is hardly surprising that his health gave way under the strain. In 1737 he had had financial anxieties, and he no longer enjoyed the resilience of youth to support him. Now well into middle age his robust health failed him. A mild form of thrombosis struck him down in the spring, and he was perilously near to a nervous breakdown. He went away to Aix-la-Chapelle, his friends being very gloomy about his prospects, for a rest and a cure. In the autumn, however, he was better and back in London, ready to take up where he had left off.

At the end of the year Queen Caroline, to whom Handel

was much attached, died after an operation. Handel composed one of his noblest works in her memory. This was the *Funeral Anthem*, which was performed at Westminster Abbey on December 17. Queen Caroline, friend of the great philosopher Gottfried Leibniz, retained her German outlook all through her life in England. It was fitting then, that in the *Funeral Anthem* Handel should show many German musical characteristics. He quoted a chorale melody

7.

and even went so far as to incorporate a sixteenth-century motet—by Jacob Handl (1550–91)—which was familiar to all Germans because of its traditional place in the Holy

Week liturgy at the Church of St Thomas, Bach's Church, in Leipzig.

A year later music from the *Funeral Anthem* was put into the first form of one of the oratorios on which Handel was then working. This was *Saul*, a subject urged on Handel by a number of people and one which displays his dramatic genius at its height. *Saul* is the story of a man who had enjoyed great power but who disintegrates into madness. Handel, who so lately had himself suffered severe mental disturbance, handled the theme with an understanding akin to that of Shakespeare in *King Lear*. But *Saul* is also the story of David and in the course of the oratorio the rise of the one hero is shown against the decline and fall of the other. It is from *Saul* that Handel's famous "Dead March" comes— now one of the few pieces of music which beyond all question are part of the British national tradition. While working on this oratorio Handel was also busy on another: *Israel in Egypt*. This is not the story of a man but of a nation and it is not surprising that it is largely worked out through the medium of the chorus. Pressed for time Handel did not hesitate to rearrange music by other composers, particularly of the Italian opera and oratorio composer Alessandro Stradella (*c.* 1645–82).

Handel frequently borrowed from himself. In the sketches of *Saul* there is part of a chorus which was only completed so far as the first bar was concerned. After that Handel hastily put down only the most important part of the music; in this case the chorus bass (with the words), the orchestral bass, and the kettle-drum part, all of which continue to the end of the movement. This sketch shows most vividly how Handel's imaginative mind worked: the "vex'd sea" is pictured by the uneasy triplet movement of the instrumental bass and the "tumultuous roar" of the waves by the rolls on the drums.

8

In the end there was no room for this splendid sea-scene in
Saul, but Handel made room in *Israel in Egypt* and the sketch
is worked up into the chorus "But the waters overwhelmed
their enemies".

Saul and *Israel in Egypt* were performed in 1739. So too
was the setting of Dryden's *Ode for St Cecilia's Day*. The
patron saint of music had been honoured in England on
November 22 by a celebratory Ode for many years. In 1739
Handel also published the twelve great *Concerti grossi* (Op. 6)
in which he summarised all that had happened in music
since the days of Corelli, whose form Handel here so elo-
quently employed. A year later one of the most "English" of
all Handel's works appeared. This was the delightful setting
of Milton's *L'Allegro*. Milton, a poet whom Handel read
with devotion, gave a word picture of English country life

in his poem. Handel translated this into music. It is hard to think of any work which so successfully depicts English people in an English landscape. It was a matter of finding the right notes for the words. Here is an example of Handel's lively response to picturesque words in *L'Allegro*.

9.

Siciliana

Let me wan-der, not un - seen by hedge-row elms, in hill-ocks green:

(*melody repeated by violin* →)

Here the plough-man near at hand, whis-tles o-ver the fur-rowed land.

Handel lived in London. But he knew England well. He had many friends who entertained him in their country houses. Thus at various times he would visit in Kent, in Wiltshire, in Rutland, in Leicestershire, in Staffordshire, and in Cheshire; and sometimes he would go to Bath or to Tunbridge Wells, according to the fashion of the day, to "take the waters".

In 1741 an invitation came to him to travel farther afield. It was an invitation from the Duke of Devonshire, Lord Lieutenant of Ireland, to go to Dublin.

9. *A Visit to Dublin*

ONE FEATURE OF LIFE in eighteenth-century England was a growing concern for the welfare of those in distress or otherwise in need of care—orphans, the sick, those in prison, mothers-to-be. Because of the interest and devotion of men like General James Oglethorpe, an active opponent of the Negro slave-trade, Captain Coram, who obtained the Charter for the Foundling Hospital and encouraged men of like mind to join him on the committee, and Henry Fielding the novelist and his brother Sir John who fought against many social evils in London, the age was distinguished by a fresh philanthropic movement. Handel devoted some part of his abundant energy to helping this movement, and in due course became a Governor of the Foundling Hospital. He helped to organise funds for the relief of musicians and their families who had fallen on evil days and supported the Society of Musicians that was founded in 1738, and to which he left a large bequest in his Will. In this year a statue of the great composer was erected in Vauxhall Gardens and this tribute was not only on account of the popularity of his music among all classes of society but also of his warm and generous personality. This statue now belongs to the nation and is to be seen in the Victoria and Albert Museum, London.

In Ireland there was much distress—which had caused Dean Swift to write some of his bitterest prose-works—and charities were brought into being one after another. For a number of years Handel's music had been performed at St Andrew's Church in Dublin in support of Dr Steevens's and the Mercer's Hospitals and the Charitable Infirmary. When a new Music Hall was built it seemed clear to a number of

people in Ireland that the proper thing to do was to invite
Handel over in person to give the first performance of a
work which it was hoped he might write for the occasion.
Among those to urge this were Matthew Dubourg, the
leader of the Viceroy's band, whom Handel had first met
many years before as a boy prodigy at Thomas Britton's
parties and Dr Patrick Delany, Chancellor of St Patrick's
Cathedral, who was to marry the widowed Mrs Pendarves
in 1743.

When he received the invitation to Dublin Handel, Italian
opera finally finished so far as he was concerned, was feeling
depressed and sensing some indifference on the part of the
London audiences. The thought of a visit to Ireland was the

stimulus he needed. He sought the help of Charles Jennens, the librettist of *Saul*, and together they undertook the text of a new oratorio. The idea of one on the subject of the *Messiah* had been with him for some time; perhaps since Pope had written a poem of that name, based on passages from the Book of Isaiah, in 1712. The text of *Messiah* is in itself a masterpiece, and many passages can be seen as relevant to the charities which Handel helped to benefit.

Handel's music made use (1) of Italian idioms (some passages were borrowed and rearranged from his earlier Italian duets) and in the "Pastoral Symphony" even quoted a Christmas-time shepherds' tune that used to be played in Rome; (2) of German ideas, most strikingly in the Passion music where the jagged rhythms and forceful harmonies have an expressive quality that is particularly German; (3) of the English methods—particularly in the treatment of voices—that had become part of his style. The overture, like all his overtures, follows the French pattern—except that here he did not end with a minuet:

Messiah was written between August 22 and September 14, 1741. When he had finished it he wrote another oratorio, *Samson*, the text of which was arranged by New-burgh Hamilton from Milton's dramatic poem *Samson Agonistes*.

The journey to Dublin was by way of Chester, where Handel managed to arrange a read-through of *Messiah* with the help of the Cathedral choristers. On arrival in Dublin two series of six concerts were organised. Dublin revelled in the feast of oratorios, opera excerpts, and concertos. Handel made many friends so that by the time April arrived tickets for the first performance of *Messiah*, to take place on April 13, were hard to come by. In order to accommodate the most number of people the organisers advertised that ladies should come to Neal's Music Hall without their hoops, gentlemen without their swords.

Messiah was first performed by the joint choirs (about forty singers) of the two Dublin Cathedrals, of St Patrick and of Christ Church, an orchestra led by Dubourg, and soloists brought from London. Of these the most famous was Susanna Cibber—before her marriage Susanna Arne, whom we last met ten years earlier (see p. 37). Mrs Cibber was an actress as well as a singer and Handel approved the way in which she, like all the English singers whom he now used whenever possible in place of the more temperamental Italians, did justice to the dramatic character of what she sang. Handel no longer considered that brilliance of style was all that his audiences wanted. He was right. They looked for meaning in the blend of words and music. And *Messiah* appeared to those Dubliners of 1742 to be full of meaning. That it was so was due to Handel's great dramatic genius; to his power of making people see what they were hearing. The most moving moment in the first performance of *Messiah*

came when Mrs Cibber sang "He was despised and re-
jected of men".

Handel enjoyed his nine months' stay in Ireland and when
one day he was asked to write a suite of *Forest Music* showed
his interest in the country by seeming to imitate Irish folk-
melody:

The gratitude of the people of Dublin was unbounded. One
writer put it in this way: "Perhaps the works of no other
composer have so largely contributed to the relief of human
suffering, as those of this illustrious musician."

10. *A Londoner*

DURING A LIFETIME many changes inevitably affect any community, or nation. When Handel came to England literary taste was nourished by the fine precision and sharp wit of the couplets of Dryden and then of Pope. By the early 1740's a new kind of literature was being created: the novel. In this sphere the important works were by Samuel Richardson and Henry Fielding. These works owed their reputation to their truth to life, to their connection with everyday experience. The realities of life were further emphasised by the brilliant and satirical engravings of William Hogarth.

Across this period a new force was felt in the religious life of England, for the claims of the Church of England—a self-satisfied and uncritical body at that time—were put seriously in question by the evangelistic fervour of John Wesley. By the time Handel had composed *Messiah* Methodism was a fact, and one to be reckoned with. Handel's oratorios were not directly affected by the Methodists (he did, however, set three of Charles Wesley's hymns to music —one being "Rejoice, the Lord is King"), but the attitude of some of his patrons was. Thus when *Messiah* was advertised for performance in London in 1743 some complained that to place this title on an advertisement was blasphemous. The first London performance of *Messiah* at Covent Garden was not very successful, but its reception was better at subsequent performances, after King George II had shown his pleasure in the work by standing up, and thus setting a fashion, during the singing of the "Hallelujah" chorus.

If there were doubts at first about *Messiah* there were none about *Samson*. It may be said that the former is not in the normal sense a dramatic work, whereas the latter is. Samson as portrayed by Handel appears as a great and tragic figure, and the chief supporting figures in the drama—Manoah, Samson's father, Harapha, the truculent and abusive Philistine, and Delila, Samson's wife—are all superbly drawn. This oratorio maintains a balance between the lyrical and the dramatic and between arias and choruses. It is *Samson* which contains the brilliant "Let the bright Seraphim" which was given to Handel's faithful and talented Italian *prima donna*, Signora Avolio (one of his Dublin soloists). The other singers were Mrs Kitty Clive—a star of the stage for whom Thomas Arne had composed some of his Shakespeare songs, Mrs Cibber, John Beard, an ex-chorister of the Chapel Royal and a former pupil of Bernard Gates, and William Savage, who had started his singing career as a boy by taking small parts in Handel's early oratorios. The singers who now clustered round Handel were devoted to him and the atmosphere of a rehearsal was very much like that of a family. As time went on the family atmosphere extended also to the audience, so that Handel's performances had a quality that belonged to hardly any other kind of music. This atmosphere persisted after Handel's death and may be experienced at the present day, especially at an oratorio sung in some remote village in Wales or in the north of England.

But Handel was not only concerned with oratorios. He was the chief musician not only to the royal family but also to the nation. By the 1740's the English were more conscious of nationality—in a modern sense—than at the beginning of the century. For nearly twenty years after Sir Robert Walpole had become Prime Minister in 1721 the country was at peace. This was due to Walpole's skilful diplomacy and to a national desire to keep out of European affairs. But in 1739 the country found that a quarrel with Spain had erupted into war. In the following year England was drawn into the European War over the succession to the throne of Austria, and hostilities of one sort or another went on until 1748. In 1743 a combined force of Hanoverians (George II was Elector of Hanover) and English won an unlikely victory against the French at Dettingen. In celebration of this Handel composed the *Dettingen Te Deum*. Two years later the Scots, led by Charles Edward Stuart, invaded England. Handel responded to the threat of invasion by composing "A Song made for the Gentlemen Volunteers of the City of London". Before the virtues of this patriotic piece could fully be tested, however, the Scots were turned back, finally to be massacred at Culloden on April 16, 1746, by the Duke of Cumberland. There then duly appeared "A Song on the Victory obtained over the Rebels, . . . set by Mr Handel: Sung by Mr Lowe in Vauxhall Gardens". Handel's oratorio of 1746 was the *Occasional Oratorio* which was generally accepted as in celebration of the deliverance of England from the Scottish invaders. Handel believed in law and order.

At this time a clergyman, Dr Thomas Morell, was writing the libretto for the oratorios and he wrote a letter in which he described how he and Handel worked together on *Judas Maccabaeus*. Morell brought what he had written and Handel approved or disapproved. If he approved he would sit down at the harpsichord and extemporise the music for a chorus. "I will bring you more tomorrow", said the Doctor. "No," said Handel, "something now." As always he worked at high speed. As a footnote to *Judas Maccabaeus* (which pleased the Jewish community in London since it dealt with a national hero) Morell tells us: "The plan of *Judas Maccabaeus* was designed as a compliment to the Duke of Cumberland, upon his returning victorious from Scotland." That oratorio was

and has remained very popular—even though it is by no means Handel's best.

The composer, however, knew how to catch a national mood and to recreate it in direct musical language. In 1749 he had further opportunity to show his prowess in this direction. The war was brought to an end and a Peace Treaty was signed at Aix-la-Chapelle. In celebration of this Handel composed the fine suite of pieces known as the *Music for the Royal Fireworks*. The hold that Handel had by this time—April 1749—is shown by the fact that at the rehearsal at Vauxhall a crowd of 12,000 turned up—causing a three-hour traffic hold-up over London Bridge. Handel used 24 oboes, 12 bassoons, 9 trumpets, 9 horns, and 3 pairs of kettle-drums for this work. Against the music guns fired and fireworks went off. The opening of the *Ouverture* (as he called it) of the *Fireworks* music, with everything playing, shows Handel as the supreme master of the simple and direct musical statement:

12

Larghetto

There were few public places in London where Handel's music was not heard. His works graced State occasions, and were played in the pleasure gardens. The oratorios were an annual fixture at Covent Garden, and to those already noted he had added *Joseph* (1743), *Belshazzar* (1745), *Joshua* and *Alexander Balus* (1748), *Solomon* and *Susanna* (1749), as well as the secular works in this class, *Semele* (1744) and *Hercules* (1745). Not surprisingly his health fluctuated, and sometimes his temper was uncertain at rehearsals. But his intimate friends made allowances, and wondered at the determination and unbounded energy of the man. Yet he was quite free from egotism. When audiences were small he shrugged his shoulders. If he lost his temper he quickly recovered his balance and charmed his companions with his geniality and the breadth of his smile. And he thought long about the misfortunes of others.

His greatest interest was in the Foundling Hospital.

11. *A National Institution*

SHORTLY AFTER the ceremonial performance of the *Fireworks Music* Handel, characteristically, offered to produce a concert in aid of the Foundling Hospital. A year later he directed a performance of *Messiah* in and for the foundation. He also presented to it an organ. On May 9, 1750, he was elected a Governor. Each year until the end of his life he presided over an annual performance of this work. Altogether the Hospital benefited to the extent of £7,000—a large sum of money in those days. In his Will, Handel left to the Governors a fair copy of the score of *Messiah* and a set of parts. It was in the year 1750 that the oratorio *Theodora* was first performed. This, unlike the other "sacred oratorios" was not based on a story from the Bible. It came from a legend about the early days of Christian martyrdom by the Romans, and was made into the text of an oratorio by Dr Morell. *Theodora* is a gentle work, lyrical rather than dramatic, for Handel felt it to be a beautiful and sad story: of two young lovers, Didimus and Theodora, whose lives were brought to an untimely end. Fate was their executioner rather than the Romans, whose soldiery the composer depicts with warm humour. The soldiers, once caught in a drunken mood, are described with more than a touch of realism. *Theodora* we may feel is an elegy to youth. Handel, as we have seen, felt for youth: again we see the man and the artist as one.

In 1750 Johann Sebastian Bach died in Leipzig. He and Handel had set out on their musical careers from the same starting-point. Each was a German brought up in the sober and excellent ways of German Church and civic music.

Bach, though well aware of much Italian, French, even English music, stayed in Germany, continued the great traditions of his country's—and his family's—musical past and brought them to a point beyond which no other composer could go. His great achievements were in these fields: of church cantata and the allied Passion, motet, and mass; of concerto—both the *concerto grosso* and the solo concerto; of keyboard and chamber music. He was the great master of fugue. His true stature, however, became clear long after his death; when he died he was buried in an unnamed grave.

In the year of Bach's death Handel was the acknowledged arbiter of the musical affairs of the British people. He had left a great heritage of operatic music, from which airs and instrumental movements were frequently played. His orchestral works, *concerti grossi* and organ concertos furnished models for many native composers—Charles Avison (1710–70), John Stanley (1713–86), William Felton (1715–69) and others. His oratorios had become the standard by which all other choral and religious music was judged. And they remained so for many years to come. Already in his lifetime the legend of Handel was developing. The oratorios, suiting the emotional needs of the English, were splendid material for choral singers. In the provinces, especially at the Three Choirs Festival (held in turn at Worcester, Gloucester, and Hereford), at Salisbury, Bath, and at Bristol the oratorios were settling into place in time for the great choral movement that swept the country during the later eighteenth and early nineteenth centuries.

Towards the end of the summer of 1750 Handel paid his last visit to Germany and was injured in a coach accident in Holland. Happily he recovered and came home to write yet another oratorio. This was *Jephtha*. As he wrote he found the task hard. His eyes were troublesome—at one point as he

E

marked on the score he had to leave off for the time being because he could not see—and his general health was none too good. He went to Cheltenham, hoping that a holiday would restore him. When he had returned to London Samuel Sharp, a surgeon of Guy's Hospital, operated on his eyes, and afterwards other surgeons tried their skill, but to no avail. In fact Handel was never completely blind (he was able to write his signature to the end) but so nearly so that people were deeply moved when they saw the great man in his affliction accompanying the great music that tells of the feelings of the blind Samson.

12. *Last Days*

IN HIS LAST YEARS Handel relied on John Christopher Smith (1712–95)—the son of Johann Christoph Schmidt, whom Handel had brought to England many years before. The younger Smith was one of Handel's pupils. He became a well-known composer and explored the fields of English opera (in 1754 and 1756 operas based on Shakespeare's *Midsummer Night's Dream* and *The Tempest* enjoyed some success) and oratorio. In 1754 he was appointed the first organist of the Foundling Hospital and as such took part in the performances of Handel's oratorios. Smith did as much as he could for his former master, who had no intention of allowing his gifts to waste away. The old man was still alert as ever. He took old works and revised them, dictating his corrections to Smith. The chief work to be revised was *The Triumph of Time and Truth*, which thus spans the whole of his active career.

Perhaps it was the memories that came back into a work written in 1708 that encouraged Handel to turn to a work that hardly ranks among his most important. Certainly Handel was thinking on his younger days, for we find him again in correspondence with his friend Telemann—now one of the most important musicians in Germany. Telemann had sent a letter to Handel through a visiting violinist, named Passerini, and Handel wrote back at once. Both men, although Germans, corresponded in French—the diplomatic and courtly language of the age. Knowing that Telemann loved flowers Handel sent him a collection of plants, which were, he said, "the best in all England". Another letter from

Handel to Telemann survives from 1754. In this he said how overjoyed he was to learn that a report of Telemann's death was false, and that more plants were on the way.

For the most part Handel lived his last years quietly. In 1750 he had made his Will and in the following years he added codicils to it so that others of his friends should benefit. At the beginning of 1759 he looked forward to and began to prepare for the Foundling Hospital *Messiah* performances. On March 30 he took his place at the oratorio as usual. But he did not feel well enough to attend the second performance a week later. He had made his last public appearance.

James Smyth, a Perfumer of New Bond Street—one of a number of London merchants who were friends of the composer and were mentioned in the Will—visited the old man who had taken to his bed and was clearly not going to recover. The "great and good Mr Handel", as Smyth described him, died on April 14. "He died," said Smyth in writing to Bernard Granville, "as he lived, a good Christian, with true sense of his duty to God and man, and in perfect charity with all the world."

On April 20 Handel was buried in Westminster Abbey. The service was sung by the choirs of the Chapel Royal, St Paul's Cathedral, and the Abbey. Three thousand of the citizens of London attended the funeral, and mourned the death of a friend and a great Londoner.

The passing of Handel was noticed in Halle and in the newspaper of that city the following announcement appeared on May 5. "On (April) 14 Mr. Georg Friedrich Händel, the world-famous musician, died. He was born in Halle in 1685, where his father, Mr. Georg Händel, was Court servant and surgeon to the Duke August of Saxony, the last Administrator of the former Archbishopric of Magdeburg. He has

left to his relatives in Germany the sum of £20,000." In fact
Handel's bequests to his relatives were somewhat less than
the figure here quoted, but it was, nevertheless, very considerable. It may then be seen how Handel united his
loyalties—the one to the land of his birth, the other to that
of his adoption.

13. *Continuing Fame*

WHEN GREAT MEN DIE there often follows a period in which their reputations suffer a decline. In the case of many musicians their works are neglected after death. This was not so in respect of Handel. But the emphasis laid on his oratorios during the last part of his life became even stronger and for a long time to come he was known almost exclusively by these works in Britain. This was due to a number of factors. The oratorios had become familiar, and the British were (and are) disinclined to welcome what in music is unfamiliar. They were "religious", and anything that could be thus classified was accepted as respectable. The oratorios, designed in the first place for the theatre, were taken over for church and chapel use; later they found a home in Victorian Town Halls, but principally at Christmas and Easter, when performances had some at least of the characteristics of religious ritual. They were also valuable as money-raisers for charities; there was hardly a hospital built in the late eighteenth and nineteenth centuries that was not endowed by the profits on Handelian performances.

In the hundred years following the death of Handel large choirs grew up in the industrial regions of England. Since these often developed under the influence of church and chapel musicians and since Handel's music was so congenial to choral singers it was inevitable that generations of choral singers should be brought up on the oratorio choruses. Given the singers and the tradition it was inevitable that other composers should follow the example of Handel. Thus Mendelssohn's *Elijah* was composed for the Festival choir of Birmingham, and so, too, were the great oratorios of Elgar.

It was very soon after Handel's death that the regular practice of performing the oratorios in the English provinces, in places other than those mentioned on p. 57, began in earnest. A clergyman, William Hanbury, of Church Langton, Leicestershire, organised a musical festival in his church on September 26 and 27, 1759. *Messiah* was given place of honour in the programme. Hanbury wrote about the performance as follows:

"The music, on so solemn a subject, by so good a band, was most affecting; and to see the effect it had on different persons was astonishingly moving and strange. An eye without tears I believe could hardly be found in the whole church, and every one endeavoured to conceal the emotions of his heart: drooping heads, to render the tears unnoticed, became for a while almost general, till by now and then looking about, one finding others affected in the like manner, no concealment in a little time was made. Tears then with unconcern were seen trickling down the faces of many: and then indeed, it was extremely moving to see the pity, compassion, and devotion, that had possessed the greatest part present."

The English had become sentimental about the music of Handel. Hanbury noted that his lead at Church Langton was immediately followed in Coventry, Northampton, Bury St Edmunds and Wolverhampton. After that there was hardly an English town without its Handel cult. This is shown by the list of subscribers to the edition by William Randall published in 1760. This was the first of many editions of Handel's oratorios in full score put out to satisfy an ever-growing demand that followed the composer's death.

In the course of time exploitation of the sentimentality that had so soon set in had a bad effect on the interpretation of the music. Recitatives and arias were pulled out of shape so that singers could put what they called "feeling" into them. The characteristic eighteenth-century ornaments which Handel had intended (but had not written into his scores because his singers knew the tradition and were directly instructed by him) were left out. Because choirs became very large the extra orchestral parts were added. It was not long before Handel's music was so dressed up that he himself would hardly have recognised it. And the scores of his works that were published were both inaccurate and incomplete.

Nevertheless the master's fame grew and grew. In 1784 there was a vast Commemoration of Handel in Westminster Abbey, with five hundred musicians taking part. A hundred years later the Handel Festivals in the Crystal Palace had ten times as many performers!

While enthusiasm in England grew and grew so it did in Germany and Austria. In 1771 Michael Arne, son of Thomas, conducted *Alexander's Feast* in Hamburg. A year later he directed the first German performance of *Messiah* in the same city. Mozart re-orchestrated the oratorios for performances in Vienna and his versions, especially of *Messiah*, were widely used. Great choral societies were founded in Germany, the most celebrated being the *Singakademie* in Berlin, and like their English counterparts they revelled in the works of Handel. During the nineteenth century his music became almost as popular in Germany as in England.

Handel's music exerted an influence on the musical life of America from early days, the main centre for its cultivation being Boston. Here in 1773 the English immigrant organist William Selby organised a concert in honour of the anniversary of the Coronation of George III. The programme

included an overture, the "Hallelujah" chorus, and one of the Coronation anthems. Somewhat later the leading musician in Boston was Johann Graupner (1767–1836), who had been born in Hanover. In 1815 Graupner founded a society "to introduce into more general practice the works of Handel, Haydn and other eminent composers". This was the Handel and Haydn Society which established an enviable reputation and the excellent standard of choral singing which developed encouraged the formation of many similar societies in other parts of the country.

To mark the centenary of Handel's death a statue was erected in the Market Place of Halle, subscribed for both by German and English Handelians. At the same time Friedrich Chrysander (1826–1901) inaugurated his great edition of the master's works. Chrysander consulted Handel's original scores and the copies that had been made for early performances and endeavoured to publish the works exactly as they had been written. This was not easy, for—as has been said—Handel's hasty writing is very difficult to decipher and in any case Handel made alterations between one performance and another; but Chrysander's work, spread over a lifetime, was methodical and as exact as he could make it. It will be many years before his scholarship is superseded, even though an international committee of scholars is at the present time engaged on the task of producing what it is hoped may be a final and definitive edition of all Handel's music.

In the nineteenth century Handel was turned into a great Romantic composer. In the twentieth century there has been a general attempt to perform his works in accordance with his own practice. Smaller choirs are now used. So far as is possible Handel's own orchestration is employed. The oratorios are still widely popular, but often they are presented on the stage in operatic form. At the same time the operas are returning to favour. That this is so is due to the energy of those who in the early years of this century pioneered their production in theatres at Göttingen, Hamburg, Leipzig and Halle.

The greatness of Handel has never been in doubt. It was acknowledged by Mozart, by Haydn (whose oratorios were modelled on those of Handel), and by Beethoven. When Beethoven received the volumes of Samuel Arnold's edition of Handel he pointed to the forty volumes and said, "There is the truth." The opinions of these masters of music have been endorsed by hundreds of thousands of music-lovers all over the world. But respect for the composer is combined with affection for the man. Above all composers Handel seems to survive in a personal way. In knowing his music we feel that we also know him. That this is so is partly due to the facts, as well as the legends, that have become generally known about his life. But it is in greater measure due to the conviction that he had—as Matthew Arnold wrote of Chaucer—"a large, free, simple, clear yet kindly view of human life."

Index